G000150794

Dear Dominic

Happy Christmas

Love from

Santa

x

Boobadoodle

Introduction

My boobadoodling first started a couple of years ago when I'd forgotten to buy my boyfriend an Easter card. I didn't have time to go to the shops, so I decided to draw him a card. Rather than use the conventional paper and pen method, I thought I'd draw a picture on my body. All I had to hand was my make-up bag so, using a mirror, I drew a chick on my breast with the beak of the chick to hide the nipple. When I showed him my masterpiece I started jumping up and down saying 'tweet tweet' to make it jiggle. I'm sure it entertained me more than him…

A few months later, I drew him a dog and every now and again I'd draw another doodle and slowly but surely the number grew. I had such fun!

There were mixed reactions when I showed the pictures to friends (probably showing it to work colleagues, including my boss, during an evening dinner was not one of the smartest things I've ever done). But it made me wonder whether other people might find this mildly amusing or even be interested in doing these themselves. After much deliberation I decided to assemble the pictures and make a book and Boobadoodle was born.

The pictures are naive and simple and all are done using make-up and a mirror. Think of this as a 'how-to-draw' book for adults! I'm not an artist (as I'm sure you'll have guessed), so if I can do them then anyone can.

My boobadoodles were scrutinised and judged by four people in-the-know plus my friends, and what follows in these pages are the ones that made the cut. We all had different favourites and hopefully you'll find one or two you'll like.

This book was a few years in the making and I have far too much evidence of the effects of gravity on my breasts than I'm comfortable with. However, I have made my peace with that and my advice to all you young ones out there is not to go dancing without a bra, no matter how small they are.

Enjoy the book and happy doodling.

Rosy Sherry

What you will need:

- Mirror (pretty essential if you're drawing on yourself, unless you're super-coordinated)

- Black and brown eye-liners: the best eye-liners are kohl or other soft ones. Sharpen them and then soften the tip with your fingers

- Red lip-liner

- Eye-shadow. The more colours, the merrier

- Talcum powder – if you don't have a matt white eye-shadow

- Wet-wipes to erase mistakes

- Cover-up stick or fluid (especially handy for people with dark nipples like me)

- Tweezers: to pluck nipple hairs if you have hairy ones like me. Otherwise keep them to add texture!

- And last, but by no means least, a pair of boobs!

Getting started:

Use the brown eye-liner as if it was a pencil and you were drawing a sketch. Do a very pale brown outline until you get it roughly how you want it (it's easier to rub off than black). Draw light lines to help get the picture just right and also to make it easier to draw over at the end. I used to have to sketch a lot on my boob in the beginning until I got more coordinated. When you're happy with the shape, go over the lines with dark brown or black.

Partners, if you're the doodler, try drawing some lines on your hand to start with. Generally eye-liners mark really easily so there's no need to press hard!

Colour in with the eye-shadow. To keep the bold outline, be careful with your colouring in! Otherwise, re-do the outline at the end. I used to find this really tricky as going back over your own line in a mirror is surprisingly fiddly.

Don't worry if you make any mistakes – use a wet wipe to rub off. Let the skin dry before drawing on the skin again.

It's not as hard as you'd think to draw on yourself using a mirror, but the more symmetrical pictures e.g. chick, yo-yo, mouse, spider and pig are easier to draw, I find, and good ones to start with. Some people have naturally good coordination – I'm not one of them. But once you start, it gets easier with practice, so don't give up! Remember this is silly fun and not an exercise in perfection.

I think the best pictures are the ones where the nipple has a real purpose rather than just drawing on your boob for the sake of it, but feel free to do that too if that's where your imagination leads you.

Have fun, be creative, and be proud of your lovely breasts.

Just Monkeying Around

I love monkeys and have always been fascinated by their intelligence. I've always wanted a pet monkey that would cling onto me and we'd go for walks together. That is never going to happen so I'll settle for this instead. He's a curious little thing and I imagine him pooping in my wardrobe and hiding in the cupboard under the stairs.

Taking the Mickey

There is possibly something a little wrong about drawing a cartoon character onto a boob, but who cares?!
I found this one a bit tricky and I think it was a complete fluke that it came out semi-decent, but there you have it.

Kung Hei Fat Choy!

One of my earliest memories was going to Chinatown and seeing a Chinese dragon – it was so impressive! I went to China in my travelling days and would love to go back. In the Chinese zodiac I'm a dragon, but I really don't feel like one. It means I'm supposed to be in a position of power! Oops.

Respect My Authoritah!

Cartman's so cute and he is really easy to draw. He looks like such a good boy in this picture, I feel I'm almost misrepresenting him!

A Sweet Treat

Cupcakes were the reason to go to birthday parties when I was younger (well, they were for me). I just loved all the different colours and toppings. We'd have such fun decorating the ones we made at home with hundreds and thousands and silver balls and I'm so glad they're fashionable again. I love how this cupcake seems to overflow over the cupcake paper. Your partner may want to eat it as it looks so good, so just remind them not to bite too hard.

Are You on the Naughty List?

I believed in Santa Claus for absolutely ages – a lot longer than any of my friends (though I never admitted that to them). It surprises me now to think that the only evidence I needed was a half-eaten mince pie and an emptied glass of sherry to think he was real!

This Father Christmas looks so festive and would make an excellent card for anyone you wouldn't mind seeing your breasts! So easy to make as he can have any shape face. You can colour in with talcum powder for a nice white fluffy beard and tash. For a 3D effect, you can use boob tape and stick on cotton wool, or use spray-on whipped cream…yum! Use red or pink eye-shadow or if you don't have those colours, you can use lip-stick or lip-liner. Ho ho ho.

Incy Wincy Spider

Halloween is such a fun night – getting dressed up and getting loads of free sweets and chocolates, what's not to love? This doodle is so easy and effective, and you can draw on both boobs for added effect. Draw the web first, starting at the nipple, then add the spider. The nipple will form the body, and then draw its eight legs. Easy! If you can't draw a spider, then use a plastic one like I did. Cheating never harmed anyone!

Cowabunga, Dude!

Bart looks so uncharacteristically innocent here. Maybe I don't know how to draw naughty? You could change his smile and the position of his eyeballs to make him look more naughty or mischievous.

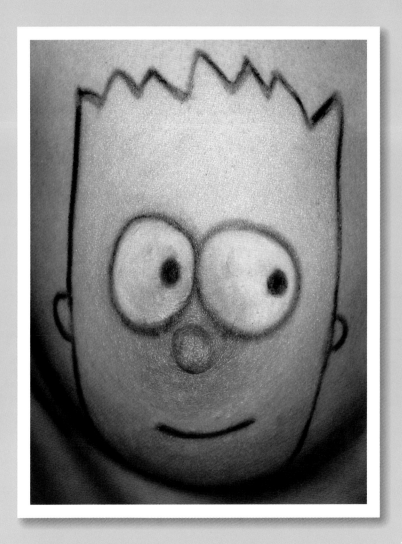

Boobushka

Such a space-saving idea, five dolls for the space of one.
I've used blue here, but you can really go all out with
colours for this one.

Funny Bones

Another Halloween-themed doodle. I used talc to fill this as my white eye-shadow is a bit too bling for a skull! The nostrils are best placed just above the nipple to get that ridged effect. Draw the other features around the nose. Again, this isn't an exercise in perfection, and if you find a better/easier picture to follow on the web or in a kids' drawing book, then do use that instead.

SpongeBoob
SquarePants

I love Spongebob! I especially love how eternally
positive he is and that he's such a perfectionist. He
just never seems to get put off or feel dejection when
criticised and I think that must be such a lovely way to
be. However, you don't have to be a perfectionist when
drawing him as he's wonderfully easy to draw. Start
with the eyes and make a goofy smile and then do the
squiggly bits around his face. No matter how well or
badly drawn he is, everyone will know who it's meant
to be!

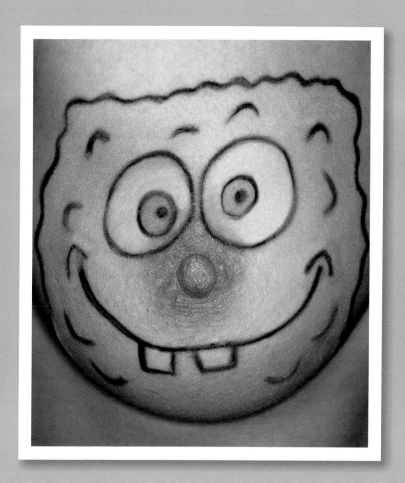

The Riddle of the Sphinx

I've been to Cairo a couple of times and always find the pyramids and sphinx an amazing sight to behold. You're probably not going to make this one into a card, but you could always create a calendar of your travels, or do a themed calendar of Wonders of the World for your partner.

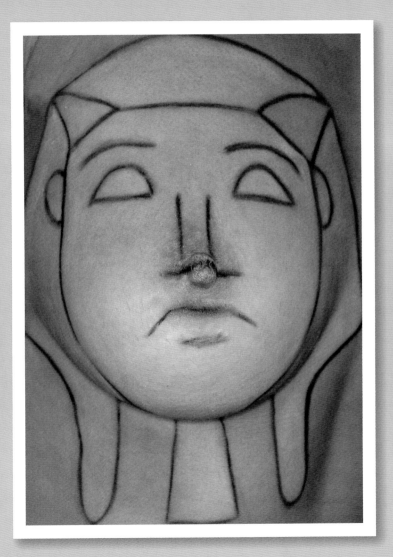

Come Fly with Me

I would love to fly in one of these planes. I imagine
myself to be a brave solo lady flying through the skies,
my knotted hair flicking painfully onto my face and
insects splattering against my goggles. Bliss.

Boob & Ernie

I loved *Sesame Street* when I was growing up and always felt so calmed by Ernie. I really thought that he was real and was looking out for me – teaching me life lessons and making sure I was OK. I think he looks a bit droopy-eyed in this, like he's about to fall asleep.

Star Signs

These doodles would make great birthday cards or a fab calendar for your close friends! Copy these or draw any picture you can find that could represent each sign. If you gather eleven friends you can draw one on each person (including yourself) and collectively make a calendar that you can all have a copy of. A great bonding experience and the best way to vanquish inhibitions. You can then turn it into a game by asking others to guess whose boob is whose!

Capricorn
Characteristics: Successful and hard-working

Aquarius

Characteristics: Independent and humanitarian

Pisces
Characteristics: Imaginative and sensitive

Aries
Characteristics: Energetic and active

Taurus
Characteristics: Reliable, loyal and caring

Gemini
Characteristics: Versatile and intelligent

Cancer
Characteristics: Emotional and nurturing

Leo

Characteristics: Warm, loving and generous

Virgo
Characteristics: Analytical and neat

Libra

Characteristics: Happy-go-lucky and sociable

Scorpio

Characteristics: Passionate and determined

Sagittarius
Characteristics: Optimistic and friendly

Mousecapades

I've had evidence of mice in my house before and thought I'd be scared if I ever saw one, but they're such cute little creatures. If I wasn't obsessed with infections and hygiene I'd have them running around everywhere. I feel bad for not wanting them in my house. I love their cute little noses and delicate little bodies, and for this doodle I borrowed my friend as she has lovely pointy nipples which make a perfect nose tip. My editor Briony thought this looked rather phallic.

I have done this one on myself and it does look cute no matter the size of nipple, but having small areolae helps so you don't have to cover them up with concealer.

Up, Up and Wahey

I've always been fascinated by balloons and amazed by how quickly and easily they can turn a place into a party venue. Now your boobs can be the place to be with these balloon doodles (maybe not at a children's party though). You'll turn any room into an instant party venue. Draw balloons of different sizes and shapes. Then colour them in and add a small stroke of white to each to make it look like the light's reflecting off them.
A colourful treat for any eye.

Hamming it Up

I've never really wanted a conventional pet like a dog or cat, but would absolutely love a pig. I'd put a pink collar on it and take it with me to the grocery shop and it would have a big garden to run around in. If you have nice pink nipples, you won't have to colour in the head! Lucky you.

Witchcraft

You can draw a witch sitting on a broom with the nipple being the nose, or you can make the nipple the wart like in this picture. She's not very scary but she's grown on me!

Get Your
Chicks Out...

This was the first doodle I ever did and it's still one of
my favourites. Draw a rough beak to cover the areola
with the nipple in the middle. Then draw a big circle
softly in brown. Colour the beak in with orange or red
eye-shadow, and the rest in yellow or gold. Then draw
little wings and instead of drawing the outline do lots of
little lines to show the fluffy feathers.

The Big Top

I've never really been scared of clowns but I can see why someone would – not this one though. This could possibly be used to help a partner over their fear OR they could then develop a fear of breasts! Hmmm, could go either way. Be as creative as you like with this one – hair, no hair, hat, bow tie (real or drawn), girl, boy ... endless options.

´Allo ´Allo

I can almost smell the garlic around his neck. I bet being associated with garlic isn't at all annoying for the French, not! You can draw the moustache or stick a fake one on like I did for added texture.

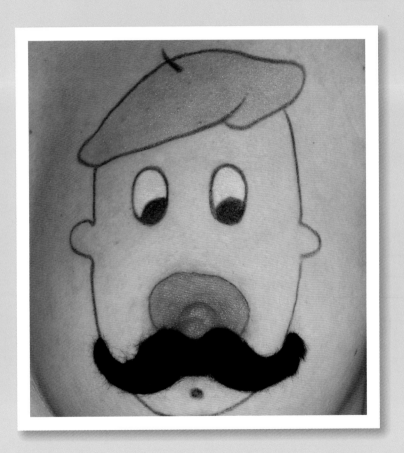

Ice to Meet You

Building snowmen continues to give pleasure to all generations throughout the ages. It's one of those simple pleasures in life that's free and accessible to all as long as you can bear being out in the cold. I love seeing other people's snowmen to see what their imagination compelled them to design.

You can change this one as much as you like by giving him a different nose or a hat, or a variety of accessories. When drawing the body, try not to twist round to look at the mirror as otherwise the picture will be a bit skewed, but maybe that's no bad thing! You may need someone to help you take a photo of this one. Perhaps do it in a chilly room to give you an erect nipple for a nice long carrot nose.

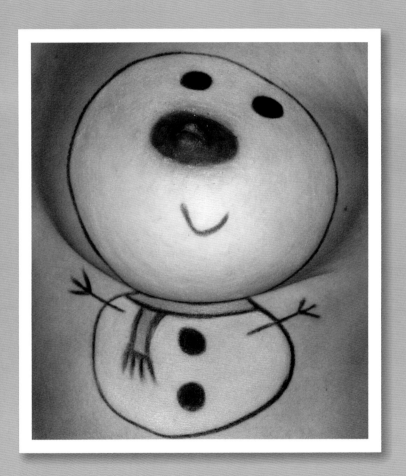

3. 2. 1. Bras Off!

I'm fascinated with outer space, and going to the moon is on my bucket list. I'd love to see the stars and planets. I wonder whether Mr Branson would exchange a free space flight for one of these books … I might ask him.

This could make a great card with a cheesy caption like 'Your love sends me to the moon' or something equally bad. You could use it as a birthday card but maybe not for your nephew!

Coming Out of My Shell

I have always wanted a big garden and with every garden come snails. My friend had some in hers and cunningly moved them into her neighbour's, but they eventually made their way back, like very slow homing birds!

A flat nipple is better for this one and will be the starting point for the shell. You could draw this for your partner if you feel the relationship is moving too slowly and you want to make a point – a nice subtle hint I think.

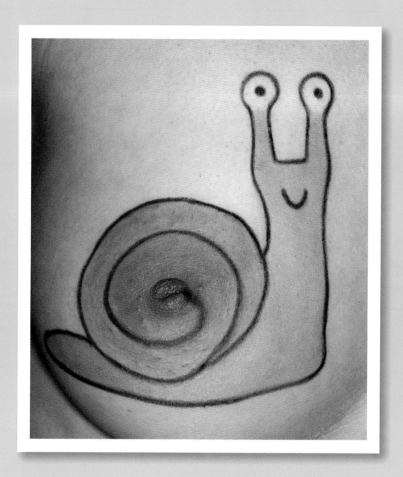

Intercity 125

My favourite form of travel is by train. I went on many trains while I was travelling the world but my favourite journey has to be on a very overpacked 3rd class train in India where we got chatting to some lovely locals sitting near us who shared their food with us then welcomed us to their home. Train travel seems to stimulate conversation and knock down boundaries somehow, and then it all disappears when you step off, like it never really happened.

Be My Valentine

I used to dread Valentine's Day when I was at school.
I'd never get a card, so I'd send myself one. But I'm sure
everyone knew as I didn't bother trying to disguise my
hand-writing. This doodle is an easy Valentine's picture or
card for your partner or date. This one's really easy to
draw and can be just as effective when not coloured in if
you don't have time.

Bouncy Bouncy

I used to love playing with yo-yos when I was young. I was only ever good at making them go up and down and couldn't do any fancy tricks with them. I like the old-fashioned wooden ones the best! If you have droopy boobs, you could jump up and down for a yo-yo type effect!

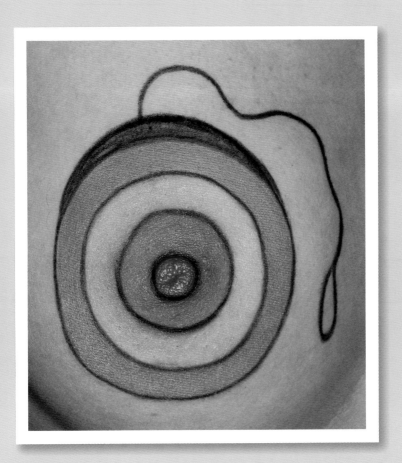

Easter Funday

Decorating Easter Eggs when I was younger was a day-long thing and such a lot of fun. I used to enjoy blowing out the egg and getting dizzy, then washing it out and painting it with paint that was so watery it would leave drip marks all over it – but we didn't care!

You can be really creative with this one, and it doesn't matter the size of the breast or the position of the nipple as the design can be adapted.

The Holly
and the Ivy

This is one of the easiest boobadoodles and when done on both boobs can look very festive indeed! This works best on small breasts with a high nipple, but can be adapted to any size and shape! Start at the nipple, drawing the berries (the actual nipple being one of them) using a brown liner to do the outline, and colour in using red lip-liner/lipstick. Then draw the holly leaves in the spaces. I start at the nipple and draw out to avoid ending up half-way through the leaf before realising that I've run out of space. To help guide you, you can mark a dot where the tip should be. This probably all sounds very basic, but it took me a while to figure out.

Honey Bunny

I really like this doodle. I drew it on myself and it worked well, but one of my friends has lovely large boobs with nice flat nipples so it worked so much better on her, creating nice big rabbit ears. She has kindly let me use the picture in the book. This is an ideal one to take a photo of, or otherwise, lie in bed with your head facing the door so it's the right way round when your loved one walks in!

We All Scream
For Ice-cream

Ice-cream is such a wonderful thing. It makes you feel
like a child, especially when served in a cone and eaten
in a park or on a beach. Takes you right back to a more
innocent time. You can use cream instead of make-up if
you prefer to encourage licking.

Ze-BRA

Zebras remind me of safari in Africa. I have such wonderful memories of my travels there – the amazing scenery, wonderful warm and welcoming people and incredible food.

You can do the zebra's face, or a derriere view like I've done. Draw the body first and all the black stripes. Next, draw the neck and a smaller head at the end to get the sense of perspective. Add all the extra bits, then colour in with white eye-shadow or talc. If you manage to avoid colouring over the lines, you won't have to go back over them at the end. I love how the nipple hole forms the perfect bum! Pure class.

Why Does It Always Rain On Me?

I had to borrow my friend for this as she has the most perfectly shaped breasts. When I drew it on myself it looked a bit wonky, but on her it came out just right.

The perkier the boobs the better, I'm afraid, droopy-boobed ladies, but there are plenty more options in the book if you're not blessed with perky breasts.

Woof, Woof

These turned out to look more like guard dogs than nice friendly ones, but I think they're fun just the same. My boyfriend's parents have dogs and they're so beautiful. They're so calm and loyal you can't help but love them.

Jingle Boobs

The idea for this picture was taken from a London Underground advertisement – which just shows you can get inspiration from anywhere! Colour it all in if you like or just colour the nose in with lipstick or lip-liner!

Lovely Darts!

My boyfriend has always wanted a dart-board. I'm thinking of blowing this picture up and backing it onto cork as a present for him.

Again this one is quite fiddly, so don't be too hard on yourself. Once you finish this you really should take a picture to have some evidence of how you spent your morning!

Close Encounters of the Boobadoodle Kind...

I'm one of those people who is convinced that there are other life forms out there. This is what I imagine them to look like, and when they speak, their skin glows. I would love to meet one as long as I didn't get hurt or have anything implanted in me.

In my head the alien speaks Spanish and says 'Ola' every time I see it. You can make yours any face/shape/colour you like. Drawing this made me feel like being a child again, when you can let your imagination take over.

Acknowledgements

Firstly thanks to my wonderful boyfriend for taking endless photos of my boobadoodles until the early hours of the morning without complaint; and for your endless support and help with the book, especially the title! You're just swell and I love you.

Thanks to my beautiful family for everything they do, especially my sis for all her help and brainstorming sessions.

Thanks to my gorgeous friends for their enthusiasm and for lending me their lovely boobs. You're all super!

Thanks to the team at Random House who've been so supportive and for thinking my silly idea could make it as a book!

Lastly and most importantly, thank you for buying this book. I really hope you enjoy it.